THE ESSENCE OF LIFE, LOVE LETTERS TO CHRIST

POEMS OF LIFE AND LOVE FROM THE PAGES OF THE HEART

TRACY A. NORRIS

J. MERRILL
PUBLISHING

ISBN: 978-1-950719-21-1 (Paperback)

ISBN: 978-1-950719-23-5 (eBook)

Library of Congress Control Number: 2019919029

Any references to historical events, real people, or real places are used fictitiously. Names, characters, and places are products of the author's imagination.

FIRST printing edition 2019.

J Merrill Publishing, Inc.

434 Hillpine Drive

Columbus, OH 43207

www.JMerrillPublishingInc.com

I dedicate this book to those that felt as though life experiences came and went without assignment and purpose. Beloved, God's word quotes in Jeremiah 29:11, "For I know the thoughts that I think towards you, says the Lord, thoughts of peace and not of evil, to give you a future and a hope."

Romans 8:28, "And we know that all things work together for good to those who love God, to them who are the called according to his purpose."

Philippians 1:6, "Being confident of this very thing, that he who began a good work in you will perfect it until the day of Christ Jesus;" Be encouraged and allow God to release your remarkable testimony that screams overcomer through "The Essence in Life, Love Letters to Christ."

INTRODUCTION

"The Essence of Life, Open Love Letters" is finding the true meaning of it and allowing it to speak poetically. Each poem tells my story of longing and finding the true essence of my being. It speaks to the heart and soul that has walked the journey called experience graduated to wisdom. I hope that this book of poems will speak to the places of your heart that have never been touched. That inner beauty, boldness, confidence, courage, and firmness will speak your name loudly for you to embrace completely.

Your journey is not in vain. It has purpose tied to it, filled with beautiful untold meanings that only you hold the key to unlock. "The Essence of Life, Open Love Letters," I release to you the pages of my heart through poetry.

CONTENTS

A PROMISE TO MYSELF

Today I make a vow to myself
I promise myself
I will always be myself
The woman God created will come forth
All of me will forever stand up tall
I am beautiful
I am smart
I am gifted
I am talented
I am loved
I have been chosen
And all of me is needed in this time
God made me who I am
He is pleased with me
I am loved by him
Today I make a vow to myself
I promise to always do right by me
To never look down on myself

To never give up on myself
To never stop believing in myself
In myself
I am more than enough I said
I AM Myself
So, today I make a vow

A TIME

One day at a time
      Just one day is fine
With each day at the same time
You'll get there in time
Without delays
Without detours
No hassle
No rush
All in the exact plan in time
In due time
It will be a lifetime of nothing more than peaceful times
You'll look back over time
And wonder
How you made it all the time
Not just sometimes
Nor a few times
But many times, you fell on hard times

Not realizing it was working out for a greater time
Oh, what a short time
That once felt like a long-lifetime
I can appreciate this sweet time now
Because I remember my wartime

ACCEPT YOU

*A*mong the few that wouldn't be placed among the top ten
    You wanted them to notice you
You desired them to make you feel apart
But the truth is this
You were always at the top
You couldn't see it till they walked away
Then you took the first step towards becoming
You became what they doubted
You endured what they gave up on
You are the resurrection of new life
The hope to a dried-out generation
Accept yourself
Love yourself
You are what they need
They just can't see it yet
So, accept what you cannot change
Accept you

ALWAYS LOVED YOU

*C*ount back all the ways I showed you that I loved you
  The many times I ran out to hold you when they told
you lies
  How long will you keep leaving my side?
  Why won't you just abide
  In the place, I've always resided
  I ride high above all of life's tides
  Can't you see I've never told you no lie?
  I've always done right by your side
  But you would rather be on the other side
  Always chasing a lie
  Never fully satisfied
  How long will you keep leaving my side?
  That I've always wanted you beside, right by my side
  Where I can always see you riding high above the tide

BEAUTY

Beauty all over
       I'm beauty from the inside out
Beauty whether you tell me or not
From each strand of hair
I grow independently strong
The slantness in both my eyes gives me clear vision to glide
I am what no one can sum up nor decide
I am Beauty
My origin is beauty
And I won't take nothing on the side
Won't come beneath on any level to decide
I rise above the expectations and opinions on both sides
I am Beauty
My name is Beauty
It doesn't require any extra words beside
Together or apart it carries its own forever
From the arch to the brace
To all the curves that give a beautiful

Silhouette
Completeness and Excellences
Elegance and Perfection
Make one's head turn and wonder
Its beauty from the inside out
BY nature

BEFORE YOU GO

If you should go
　　　　I want you to know
I love you so
I loved you then
I'll love you now
Until the ages to come
When the earth stops turning on its axel
If the birds should no longer be chirping
My love will weather all seasons
My love will go on forever
I loved you so deep; I laid down my own life
How many people would give you their life?
I know this world has made you think
It was me pushing you away
I am here to stay
Always shall I remain?
Before you go

If you should go
I want you to know
I'll never stop loving you so

BELOVED THIS ONE'S FOR YOU

*Y*ou are a beautiful work of art
      Precious treasure of mine
      You hold true value at heart
There will never become another beside you
They just can't fill nor fit your style
You add to that what is missing in many
You are the missing piece to all my puzzles
The strongest link to all cords
One cannot be so easily broken nor torn apart
Most valuable piece of work dear to me
From the driest places of the earth
You came forth just as a stream
Not appealing to much
But you grew firm and upright
The capitellar evolved over time inside you
That old cocoon couldn't hold you closed tight anymore
You needed room to stretch out your colorful, majestic wings
Soar high my most beautiful treasure at heart

You are everything I've dreamt of you becoming
My eyes can now take rest
My most beautiful has taken flight at its best

This One's for you, my beloved

BETTER OFF

I'm better off now, and I think it's time for that
This is the greater version of me
No loose ends
Nor open gaps
Not even in between
Nor mishaps
I'm not chasing
No calling cards
Not forcing me to fit into your clickish flick
No repeats
Nor hang-ups
Head up, chest out and shoulders back
Confidence stands upright just like that
A hard head will always make a soft bottom
Momma always said, "don't take no wooden dollars"
So, I'm better off now, and that's a fact
She didn't raise no fool

I won't play any part of being your tool
What's yo aim child, whatcha want out of life
Cause need I remind you
You're better off without them than that

BLINK

I blinked, and you vanished
     I looked away only for a second, and you disappeared
The day I lost you
My body ran numb
My thoughts stood still as the rest of the world moved around me
My heart and mind tried its best to will you back
Countless hours
Sleepless nights
Am I dreaming?
Is this really happening
Why
How long will this feeling last
When will it leave me?
I didn't see this coming
What page did I miss in your story?
I'm sorry I don't recall us departing this way
I heard one say here today gone tomorrow
Why tomorrow

And not years later
Unprepared
Unrehearsed
Unexpected
You took flight
Exchanged earth with heaven
Oh, how I miss you
And tomorrow I'll miss you even the more
I blinked, and my world changed forever

BUTTERFLIES DANCING HIGH

Butterflies dancing in the sky
  They come to me all one at a time
Helping me to find my true beauty inside
That lies from behind all my cries
Butterflies dancing in the sky
It's my guardian angel singing back to me
She tells me that all my tears have created a rainbow
The sun has shined brighter upon me
My butterfly sings louder for me
Beautiful butterflies dancing in the sky
She's what gives the melody it's harmony
In a circular motion
Rays of colors
They each will soar high for me
Butterflies dancing in the sky
The dawning of my new morning is approaching
The strong tide in the waves refreshes me
My morning sun pushes back the heavy clouds

Rains lose grip in strength
Noisy winds turn away her power
My butterfly dances in the sky for me
I have emerged from my cocoon
My wings have fully matured
They are ready to soar among the heights
I am dancing in the sky
I have uncovered my beauty in the pain
My tears birth colors of strength
I am surrounded by love
Enclothed with soundness of mind
I am safe there
Beautiful dancing in the sky with me

CAUGHT UP

*C*aught up
　　　Never to repeat
People, places and times
All deceit and full of secrets that lied
The truth stands on its own
It needs neither handle nor stick for firmness
Just a matter of time
In due time like they say
When one grows sick 'n tired of lies
All fantasies must come to a ties end
They come tumbling down all at once
Like a tower without foundation to support
Deception and lies
Like a bird caught and caged at one time
Read between the lines
Pay attention to the signs
It tells no lie
Only for those that want to hide

Pulled away from what really mattered
Distracted
Pushed to the edge
Let go is what's screaming on the inside
Fly alone and high is what's pushing in
It tells me don't get caught up this way again

CHANGE

A lot of things change as you get older
Some say change is good
I say change is, well it all depends
Change of faces, change in routines
Change in lifestyles, just simply change
All the ever to get used to
Difficult at first
Minor adjustments of change
I have seen it in many ways
Take its toll on some not to be rehearsed
Change is inevitable
It does not need your consent
With or without it joins at your waist
It will meet you along the side
To exchange with you a different way
Hello, my name is CHANGE, pleasure to meet you

CREATE YOUR MOMENT

*S*he said nobody taught her how to fly
      Extend your arms and run towards your purpose
But this time don't fly
SOAR
She felt like she wasn't given the opportunities as others
Don't ever wait for someone to hand you a moment
Create moments and make them memorable
LEGACY
Skyscrapers across your mind
You are as great and powerful as you think
It's better caught than taught
Now pay close attention
What's inside you must come out of you
The sky is not the limit
You can soar higher if you dare to believe

DON'T HOLD BACK

*W*hy keep quiet
Forever holding back
Let the best of you step forward
Push yourself from out of that corner
Let the real version of you finally exhale
Who are you waiting on, really
Last time I checked, they weren't coming back
So get up and brush your shoulders off
Wipe the dust from your knee caps
You still got work to do
A mission to complete
Your destiny to fulfill
Don't need no more confirmations than what you started out with
You are the best version of yourself
Tell your story like it is
Forget about the applause and approvals of men
Let words flow like water off the pages to the hearts of many
Don't Hold Back

DON'T WAIT ANOTHER DAY

You waited one day too long enough
If not now, when
In one day missed another day appeared
The sun comes up one day
Another day it will do just the same
Stop waiting for the right day
The right time
The perfect moment
That one day will never come again
It will not reappear once more to take
Take advantage of the time that has been granted to the day
It's your day, if you want it that way
Your time
On this day
The perfect moment
Without words
Put all that in action

Now watch the day work for you
Not another day wasted
Because you choose not to wait another day

EMBRACING ME ALL IN 1

*L*iving my life courageously
   Out loud
   On purpose
With God
Without regrets
No repeats
Please don't compare
Never apologize for becoming your authentic self
Not here to please
Didn't show up for the applauses
Just truly embracing me
The way God spoke of me
Then turn around gave it life
I wouldn't want it any other way
Some copy my DNA
No, I don't think so, please
You were given your own blueprint
Embrace it

Love you
There won't come another after you
Someone else needs to see the strength in you
They want to feel alive once again
So, embrace you, and they embrace themselves
All in 1

EVERYTHING ABOUT YOU

*E*verything about you is amazing
Everything about you is wonderful
Everything about you is unique
Everything about you is a masterpiece
You're not a carbon copy
You're not an imitation
You're original
Extraordinary
Its time you start believing that
From the top of your head to the soles of your feet
You're perfect
So, stop 2nd guessing yourself; it's time you start believing in yourself
You're Everything

FAMILY

Family is
        Family does
What you make of it
What you won't
All the same
But took different paths to claim
They say loves never dies
Only gets stronger has the days go by
Yes unpredictable
Changing lanes all too quickly
Why can't things just remain the same?
Age gauges different from within
Moves quicker in time
Some never come to appreciate until it's gone
My how times flies
We look up and watch how family goes by
Family dies off
New family is born

All to hold near
Let us cherish every moment that we may lose that is dear
What used to be?
What is it that draws us close?
Binds us
Keeps us
It is family that remains close

GET UP FROM THERE

Climb out of that bottomless pit
Stop playing the victim
Mamma didn't raise no fool
What's wrong with you?
Clean up this room
Pick up all these torn pages
And unrehearsed lines
Empty thoughts
That left you clueless and lost
This feeling of being left behind and stuck
You need to be smarter next time
Next time
For a moment of being spaced out
Wondering what will happen next what's my next move
Don't make it a long road to recovery
I'll be wiser next time around
They didn't stick around

Feeding me rhymes for riddles
Don't hand me no bag of pebbles
Can't you read within between my lines?
I need to be smarter this time
Not playing their fool

HE SAID HE DID

*H*e said he loved me
>> *But his actions were only to take from me*
They say love is warm
It's like a charm
It knows no harm
So why do I keep feeling like this is all so wrong
I tried to guard my heart, but it got too hard
I found myself in the game played like tossing cards
Too weak to speak
Unable to seek about a way out
What do I do?
I'm too far in, lost in the battle from within
This is all the same, but really, I'm to blame
Sometimes up
Other times down
I'm tired of him being around
He ain't changed
He still acting strange

Got me all mixed up and disarrange
I just wanna change
He's on a different plane
I need to be in my own lane
And stop stooping low taking blow after blow
He must know that it's time for him to go
His ways are so old, and I'm sick of being left in the cold
I've been told I shine like gold
I'm ready to let go of this stronghold
Just be bold
And forget about what he said and whatever he did

HIS WORDS, YOU CREATE

*W*ords create feelings
 And feelings are not always accurate
Somewhere in between, they met
Life danced with the universe
The Lord spoke a Word and gave birth to everything
The bitter
The sweet
The good
The bad
The outcome is a matter of choice
A choice to live by God's Word and give birth
It will determine how sweet and bitter will even out
From the words we create
Feelings follow behind it closely
And who's to say if it's accurate
Only time will tell how it all evens out
Words create feelings
And in time we shall witness what it brings forth

I AM HE AND YOU ARE MINE

From a bud to a flower
   I started out as a seed
My roots run deep
My branches stretch far and wide
Who am I
I am a tree
I give rest to the weary faint indeed
God said to me
I am He
I come in the volume of the book of life
I am that I am
The bread of life
The living water that never runs dry
Come unto me; you are weary and faint
This I see
My word is the roots in the tree
My love stretches far and wide for you
You will never hunger nor thirst again

You are the seed sayeth the Lord I planted
You've emerged from the bud to a radiant flower
Stay connected to the roots of the tree
For I give life
I am He, and you are mine

I AM HER

*C*ome out
       Come forth
  Let thy voice be heard
  Make known to the ones that sit in fear
  That think in doubt
  They need to hear of your strength
  Your life after death
  The depth in your tone was where strength spoke up
  The words that were released was the place we understood wisdom
more clearly
  Stand tall, stand upright
  Let thy posture declare firm foundation
  You are what you think in your mind to be
  Come away from the shadows
  Come out from hiding
  These people need to see
  This generation dies to hear

TRACY A. NORRIS

I Am Strength
I Am Her

I AM HERE

I am here my dear
        Take my hand, let me lead you in
No need to fear
I'll always be here
Today, tomorrow and forever
Where will you go?
Who will give you shelter
Haven't I always been your refuge?
I am here
Never to abandon
Not to tare down
Let me hold you
Build you up
Show you what real love is all about
My voice heals
My hands comfort
My correction transforms
I am here

Let me come in
Into the place you hide in fear
Reveal unto you why I am here
I am here
I am here
Always near
You can count on me
No need for fear
Because I am here

I FINALLY SEE HER

I see myself in that girl
Please tell her to hold on to her
She came to far to turn back now
Hey, I see myself in that girl
She's stronger today than she was yesterday
Please tell her not to let go of her
Remind her of her value and worth she gracefully carries
Tell her to be courageous in the fight for her life
Remind her that many look to her for refuge and strength
Tell her to hold on just a while longer
Her breakthrough is just about near
Never mind the ones that cast her aside and lied
They walked away because of her deep pain she cried
This is where her destiny resides
Her purpose is revived
Her pain will become her gain
Those tears will be her laughter

If you don't remind her, I'll speak to her myself
Who is that girl looking back at me?
It is I
I have survived

I STILL MATTER

*B*ehind the frame tight fitted faces
     Broken stone-like hearts
Mixed up and confused emotions; that raise the question
Do I Still Matter, yes you do
I Still Matter
Lost and left behind
Overlooked so many different times
Till no one could even find
I Still Matter
The fact that you died and then rose back up
Screams I Still Matter
Not a waste
Never in vain
Worth it all
Purchase by his blood
Yes, I Still Matter
The significance and uniqueness you spoke into me said
Yes, I Still Matter

Not defined by my past
Not graded by those that just sit and stare
Yes, I Still Matter
Not defined by the crowd of unmatched qualities
Yes, I Still Matter
Hand chosen by Christ to be placed among those
That felt the same way
Shared the same pain
Cried the same tears
All to speak out for them that said nothing at all
Yes, You Still Matter

IT WAS

It was when I was alone
        I heard your voice without noise
It was when they gave up
You said start believing CHRIST would never give up
It was when they walked away
You knocked at the core of my heart
You drew me closer and never blew me away
Every tear you caught and returned it for my laughter
You are my morning
My very daybreak
You found me at the edge of my lake
You grafted the pages of my heart back to whole
How could I ever repay you for how you have loved me?
It was when I was lost
You found me and never let go
It was how you loved me
I could never leave you ever

TRACY A. NORRIS

It was and will ever be our story of
How it was

IT'S HER TIME

It's your time
This is the moment
Curtains rolled back
Lights beam bright
Stage raised high
Give her the mic
She's ready to speak
Don't hold back
Let it all rollback
A place in time
When life looked innocent
And people sound believable
The sweet sound of victory
Music to my hears
I'm ready to shine
Let the whole world be mine
No holding back

This is my greatest comeback
Give me the mic
I'm ready to let it rip
My time
Winners take all

JUST BEING ME

*P*assing faces,
     Smiling faces,
Whose face can I really trust?
As people come,
People go but, someone will stay and be more than a passing face
Just passing by or another smiling face only to say hi
I look in the mirror and say to myself
You are more than just a beautiful face to look upon
More than a beautiful smile to match it
You got charism
You are everything Hollywood doesn't have but, desperately needs
and you better know it
Walk the walk, talk the talk and never 2nd guess yourself
The sky isn't the limit just keep reaching, and you'll see how far
you go
I am everything they didn't believe in
I am everything they didn't even see coming, like a shooting star
flash before your eyes like lighting

There I am in your face, stuck in your memory never to be forgotten

JUST ME NOTHING LESS

The coolest
     The weirdest
The strongest
Yes that's me
Nothing less but all beautiful me
Take me as I am or leave me where I stand
Just as the same
Me and nothing less
No in-betweens
No hidden doors
No riddles tales
What you see is what you get
Just Me
Yes that's me and nothing less
Poise is the way I sway
I don't settle for anything under my feet
I'm just me

Made for me
And that's the way I sway
Nothing less
Just me

JUST TELL HER

ell her the truth
Never a lie
Get it out the way
So, you'll never have to hide it on the inside
It may hurt she may even cry
But at least she'll know
How you really feel on the inside
Never looking just from the outside
You owe it to her
So, do it the right way
Make ends right
Close all gaps
Make sure they're tight
So, we never have to repeat this chapter again
This way reads right
That side reads left
The truth will always stand strong
Even in a room filled with lies

No two wrongs add up to right
The heart is too fragile to handle just right
So, tell her the truth
Make ends right
It may hurt, but she will survive
This time will be different
This time will be brand new
This time I'll awake and stay

LIVE, LAUGH, LOVE

I *have no regrets*
       I love out Loud
I found the secret to life
LOVE
It knows no wrong
It keeps no record
Cause it loves unconditionally
What I didn't know then I understand now
Life is just for a moment
Here today
Gone tomorrow
*Like the beauty of a butterfly that enters one's life, it quickly
withers*
Life is just for a moment
Cherish it wisely
Nurture it with care
Cause it LOVES out Loud

Sometimes in the craziest ways
I have no regrets
I love out loud
Because I found the secret in life
LOVE

LOVER'S REST

A moment can last forever
You can play it back whenever
For a lifetime spent
We've promised together
To death till we part
Let's cherish every moment
Our love will ride high and last for all eternity
It will withstand the rain and wind to come
It shall live out the time
We have each other
We are all we need
Nothing can tear us apart
Not ever
A moment
Our moment is forever

MEMORY

soft thought of you brushed up against me one day
As the song played, the memories unrolled
We were young and full of life
Care-free, nothing could stop us
Faster than the speed of light
Seem like just yesterday; the feeling still stayed the same
The world was ours for the asking
All our dreams at our fingertips
It was the day
It was the hour
Seconds and minutes combined together
Came and went like a blink of an eye
It was a memory so clear
I'll never forget it
To forget would be to forget you
We locked hands
In our vows we made
Never to depart

The feeling
The moment
Who would have thought we'd make it to the finish line
Our journey was sweet; it had pebbles but all the worth
Even though your journey stopped, the memory remained vivid
It will be one I'll always cherish
It was when I remembered us

MORE THAN THAT

I am more than what I've been through
The opinions of others do not define me
I am not the replica of my past mistakes
The Lord saw worth in me, while the world couldn't understand my value
Lord, you have turned my mourning into dancing
I will forever give you praise
You have made my path straight
All thy mysteries you have made known to me
I have sought after thee, Oh Lord, like hidden treasures
You are my one and only true desire
Because you told me I'm more than that
You said you are more than just a pretty face on a cover
More than a lovely voice in a tune
You're not an ideal, not even a thought
You're more than a piece to a missing puzzle
You are outstanding; you surprise them every time you show up
Not a question mark, not even the end to a period

You are outstanding in all you do
You outshine the sun in all its brightness
You were amazingly created to amaze the whole world
That's who you are and more
You bring high rays of color to all the places you walk
Now go sprinkle your shine

MOVING ON

Up/down
All-around
Just like a merry-go-round
Keeps me out of bound
I need to be moving on
This place feels so far gone
There's nothing here for me now
The place I made my vow
A home I thought was STRONG
Has now waxed cold and old
The warmth has left it
There's not a thing coming from it
Best I be moving on
I will not submit
This is my stop, yes, I'm getting off

MY LOVE

You are the dawning of a new day
The breaking away of my past
Yesterday is far behind me
The better half makes up all of me
We live our lives as a tale played out
Of course, you've already seen this twice
I'm in love with you
I'm in the thick of it
There's no between
You are the dawning of my new day
I can no longer hideaway
I won't stay away
You make up all of me

MY LOVE

*Y*ou are my one and only true love
    You threw out the love net and told me to latch on
    With your compassion and mercy, it pulled me in
I belong to you; I know my identity
Nothing is kept hidden from me
You have revealed it all to me
Your love is greater than all mankind
Your hands are stronger than any force being
You amaze me; I'm amazed by you
Your undying Love towards me
You are my true desire
My heart beats for you
You are my one and only true love
You threw out the love net and told me to latch on to it

MY PEACE REMAINS

*M*y peace you give
It is unshakeable
Unlike the world
It lasts out the ages of times
It doesn't come and leave
Mountains quake
Earth rumbles
Oceans erupt
My peace remains
People come
People go
Sometimes in with you
Sometimes not with you
My peace remains
Pain
Disappointments
Heart-aches
Sadness

My peace remains
Nothing can move me
No surprises
No pop-ups
Nothing lost
Because my peace is made strong and remains

NEVER SAY NEVER

ever say never that you'll never walk in ever
      I remember a time when I thought this would be my
forever
   Forever broken
   Forever a victim
   Forever out of place
   Forever, forever
   Until I met up with the endeavor
   It taught me how to push through whatever
   When whatever showed up
   I learned to be clever wherever
   And never lose whosoever
   I realized no matter whatever and whomever
   That, however, the outcome my forever will always stand
   Brighter than my never

NO MORE

I'm over it now
        Not revisiting that place again no more
Not remembering it no more
It served its purpose, and I'm not needed there no more
No more
No more
Will I allow?
No more will I stay
I stayed too long the last time
Said too much this time
No more will I be pushed off
No more playing the victim
No more defeated
No more insecure
No more unsure
A closed mouth won't be fed
So, no more fear

No more holding back
Take a deep breath and let it rip
With no more regrets

NO REPEATS

This is what it is
  This is how it's gone be
I'm sitting the record straight
Making my point clear across the board
Drawing a line within the sand
Not going back for another time to begin
No more repeats
I said no more repeats
We're not starting over no more
Sitting the record straight
Making my words clear like once before
I'm making my words clear like once again
But you're stuck constantly trying to figure it out once more
I'm talking about coming out
Coming out from among them
Being separated once and for all
I'm coming out and not looking back
Not putting my fingertips back in that trap

That situation nearly blinded me for a life time
That sin sandbox ain't FO nobody to play in
Hey there ain't no guarantees
No exchanges
And no returns
No Repeats

NO VACANCY

*H*e said what I won't do
Another will
Another has
Maybe even better
You wasn't the first
You sho nuff will not be the last
But I got something for all of that
Momma didn't raise no fool, and I just won't be handled as some tool
I mean c'mon now, can't you read between the lines
Or should I carve it between your thighs
No Vacancy
Do I make myself clear?
I didn't lead you on
I never told no lies
You misunderstand me
That's the reason why
No Vacancy

And I don't have to tell you why
It's on my side where the truth lies
End of story, case closed
No Vacancy
You can't stay here
Keep knocking because you'll never get in
My ways were the same just as before
I never told no lies
I never lead you on
You can't stay here
Like I said once before

No Vacancy

NOW IS THE TIME

*A*wake
     Arise
Open your eyes
Do you realize what time is on the inside?
Declare
Decree
Release the words that will set them free
Restore
Revive
They're in desperate need for refreshing rain
Define the times that we often lose sometimes
Task
Appoint
We have been given an assignment
The opportunity is now
To win
To gain
To claim victory in every plain cause now is the time

PLAYING THE FOOL

*G*et up from there
    Climb out of the bottomless pit
    Stop playing the victim
Mamma didn't raise no fool
What's wrong with you
Clean up this room
Pick up all these torn pages
And unrehearsed lines
Empty thoughts
That left you clueless and lost
This feeling of being left behind and stuck
You need to be smarter next time
Next time
For a moment of being spaced out
Wondering what will happen next what's my next move
Don't make it a long road to recovery
I'll be wiser next time around
They didn't stick around

Feeding me rhymes for riddles
Don't hand me no bag of pebbles
Can't you read what's in between my lines
I need to be smarter this time
Not playing their fool

RED BLUE SKIES

Red blue skies
　　Play across my eyes
Paint the portrait of love all in red
Red blue skies
Where has she flown off to now?
Ribbons dancing in mid-air
Who cares what it looks like?
I am flying high
I can feel the slightest breeze beneath my fingertips
Its red blue skies
Swing low
Rise high
So carefree
I wanna bask in a bed of lilies
Swim off into the streams
I'm homebound free
Never to look behind

TRACY A. NORRIS

I am released from all and in between
I am soaring above the red blue skies within

REPAIR THE BREACH

I gave her a voice that no one could keep
A mind made up that no one would steal
She speaks what many wouldn't dare to release
Authority in her voice
Strength is her walk
Powerfully unheard of
Some would ask where she came from
A place not thought of but created in the mind
Spoken in time
Sat up on high
She knows her place
She hasn't much time
So, let's begin with it
Listen, she's fine
I will show you how to mend all of the breaches in the line
Make things right within your family tide
Keep them close never let them slip away
Family is forever

Friends for a moment
It must matter
Now is the time, make it right
Don't waste another second in time
Repair the breach

SEASONS OF TIME

What I've learned today I wish I knew yesterday
But yesterday is behind me
And tomorrow is not promise to me
So, I grab hold of today and enjoy it at its best
Counting my blessings, each one at a time
Living life up to its fullest
I am a blessing in time
Spoiled milk cannot be scooped back into a jar
Why cry over what has been taken and lost forever
If it's truly meant to have let it return in time
Pyramids weren't built overnight
Mountains are climbed best at ease with a steady pace
Letting go is often the hardest than reaching ahead for tomorrow
Looking back can cause one to stumble and miss its turn
A flower doesn't bloom forever
It dies in its season and rebirths in its time
What's here today is gone tomorrow
It's never forgotten forever

The wind whistles but where has it started
The earth rotates but when does it stop
The sun rises without being told it's time to rise
The brightness of it never goes dim
We are all in the same cycle of seasons and times
What I missed out on for years
I make up for lost times
We are never behind
Never delayed nor denied
We all get there in the seasons of time
What I've learned today I'll hold for eternity

SHE KNOWS

She knows who she is
She's a go-getter
She doesn't wait for it
She creates it
The power in her words
The authority in her tone
She knows who she is
Without second-guessing
No room for procrastination
What is hesitation?
She knows who she is
Runs towards her dreams
Never away from her team
Its purpose is to transform her
It's time for her to become
Let go of your fears
Throw away those crutches

Open your mouth
Let your words create change
Cause you know who you are

THE MOMENT

*P*ivot moments in one's life
   Defining moments in others
We will all reach our destiny if we faint not
In time all moments will eventually equal up to one moment
The moment that you have been waiting for
Hoping and wishing on
Praying, for now, you have finally caught up with it
This moment waited on you
Patiently endured for you
Never changed on you
When you finally realize the moment became you
It connected and came together as one for you
No turning back
No more reliving that
This moment is just for you

THE REAL ME

When will the real me show up
            Everyone seems to be rooting for me
But why won't I believe in me
I took too many hard punches
Had to too many set-backs and mishaps
Who is the real me I ask
Was there ever a time I was being my real self
Who can I really trust?
Kinda feeling like I'm out here by myself
Like on an island alone
Gotta learn how to survive without the kit
I just got kicked out the nest
Didn't know it would look like this
Will the real me please show up now
Its look-in kinda dark over this way
Someone gotta match or at least a jacket to keep warm
Maybe that's what this being strong thang is all about

Ok I'm done playing weak and feeble
Let the real me now stand up

THE TRUTH

*I*t's the truth
    And don't try to tell it for me
It will be better to hear it from the one that experienced it
Everyone sees life from a different angle
What started off difficult?
Gradually became easy
What they tried to tear down
Only became stronger
What some attempt to destroy?
Got much tougher to withstand
Wiser today than yesterday
Better to handle than ever
The higher up, the tougher it gets
Many walked away from what now they regret
The greatest come back is when you scored at the lowest
Fallen so deep down the rabbit's hole
No one to lift you up for a helping hand
Na they to scared what they might pull out

A warrior is born within the caves
Confidence is gained in the face of fear
I am the truth
I rose up out of the dirt that you walked all over
And I'll tell my story better than anyone
It will be the TRUTH

THE VOICE

*H*er voice
   His voice
Their voice
Your voice
It tells a story
It's set apart
Unlike any other voice
No one carries your voice
It gives
It takes
It hurts
It heals
It's a voice that cannot be matched
It's yours forever no one can take
It builds
It teaches
It holds
It releases

And when it has reached its end
And has given out all from within
It relaxes
It knows
It's power

THIS IS WHO I AM

I was made to soar,
      Promised to win,
Given the authority to conquer
Chosen to lead
Who am I, I am the apple of God's eyes
I am the chosen one after God's own heart
He has never left my side
Every step that I make is guided by his hands of grace
Born with a purpose
Spoken from nothing into something greater than this world
I am God's leading lady
I only speak and operate under the obedience of one voice
Jesus
I have the eyes of an eagle
I cried tears that only God could wipe away
I carried weights that only God could lift
I Know Who I Am

WALKING AWAY, LETTING MYSELF BREATH

I'm not giving you life anymore
*   The little I gave almost took my life*
Sent me into a midlife crisis
Made me get back up and fight
This is the new me
That way was never for me
So, I'm walking away
Letting myself breath
Letting myself live again
This is not my portion
Up all night
Tossing and turning
That was never for me to carry
Never meant to be a part of me
I'm stronger than that
Better than that
Learned from that

Want better for me
So, I am walking away
Letting myself breath once again

WHAT ARE YOU, WHO ARE YOU

*B*ring your mind into the time
        Be no longer afraid
Speak the truth
Hold it not back
For it is not yours to keep back
It must be given back
Release into the atmosphere CHANGE
Change and Time have caught up with each other
Let silence no longer take up space
Wisdom and boldness have laid out her platform
I speak to an audience that has accepted the change
Occupy until the day I return
Study to show yourself ready to be used
Hold to the truth and sell it not
For what's in you must come out
What you're made of shall be revealed
I am the change that you need
I am he who holds what you want

I hold the keys to bringing you forth
The power to change
What am I, who am I
I am what you need
I am Christ

WHAT'S TO COME?

What legacy will you leave behind?
What story will be told about you?
Will you be the starter of many new things?
Or the ender of old things
The ender of what crippled your generation
The starter of what made them greater than any other nation
What's to come?
Some got lost in the battle
Some were conquered on the field
But our faith and confidence lay in Him who holds us dear
The One who has never lost the battle
So, this is what's to come
We will rise to the occasion
A generation strong with power
Walking in our destiny
Leaving a true legacy
And, this is what's to come

Will you rise to the occasion
Or just race to make your own name great
Are you a strong link in a chain leading to heaven
The voice of a generation will hear and will rise to the occasion
What's to come?

WHO DO YOU SAY YOU ARE?

When you look into the mirror every day
What do you see looking back at you?
What man or woman do you declare that you are?
Hmmm, interesting how some said I was just a woman with only beauty
Nothing more
Others thought I was just a quiet person
Trapped in my past
But know this; it's not up to them
Not what she sees or what he thinks
Not even what they say
The question really lays within you
What do you say about yourself?
How do you feel about who you are becoming?
You are what you say you are
You become what you think

WHO KNOWS THEIR WORTH?

They say what goes around comes around
       It usually comes back in another form around
What you put in life
You surely get back out of life
Don't like the backside of a dirty penny
Well change it up and make it shine brand new
I discovered my value at the bottom of the ocean that was dark blue
Where the sun doesn't reach and is too far to see for a clue
My worth became my mantle of honor
My crown in glory
Flawless and unique
Perfection at its peak
They overlooked and ignored
That which they toss overboard
Became the world's most precious value of all times
Nothing to be compared to it

They were mesmerized upon something all so rare
It came back around at its lowest apparel
A real jewel was birth at its highest value, and worth appeared

YOU ARE JUST THAT

*Y*ou're a breath of fresh air
  You came from out of nowhere
  You're a new song in my mind that is so clear
The notes we write have never been so near
You are a true melody but from where
Please stay my sweet shining knight
That glows so bright in the night
You are my prince in-flight riding high above all fights
You are just that more than that

YOU'LL KNOW WHEN

I'll let you know when
      When I come
You'll know when
Coming into
Never without
I am the first and the last
I come in the volume of the book
I stand at the gate
Will you let me come in?
Sit with you
Talk to you
Be with you
Dwell in you
I'll let you know when
When I come
I promise you'll know when

YOUR VOICE, POWER

I was given a voice that no one could silence
*   A mind so fortified that not even the strong could*
tear down
*   You have what many desire to become*
*   But refuse to step out and believe*
*   Authority in my voice*
*   Strength is my walk*
*   Some would even ask where I come from*
*   No place on the map but created in the mind*
*   Spoken out loud*
*   Strength too many*
*   Courage for others*
*   Your voice gave them power*
*   Your strength caused them to believe*
*   The power in one transferred to another*
*   You were given a voice that no one could silence*
*   A mind so fortified that not even the strong could tear down*
*   Your voice gave power*

ACKNOWLEDGMENTS

Lord, I thank you for being everything I need, more than enough, You've always provided. Thank you, most heavenly Father, for enabling me to share my testimony to millions that will be blessed abundantly through my book. Lord Jesus, I give you all praise. Without you, I am nothing and can do nothing. So, I keep you at the front and center always.

I believe that all I've experienced on this journey was never intended for me to keep inward but, to encourage many through the releasing of The Essence of Life, Love Letters to Christ. Father allow this book, each poem to reach and search out the layers in the reader's hearts and began to heal from the inside out. This, I pray and release in Jesus' name, Amen.

To My Beloved Champions

Jeitreni McCoy and Treivini Norris, you two bring out the best in me. Never abort your assignment, you were made to soar among the EAGLES. I give you the very best of me, so you both shall always believe it can be accomplished.

To My Beloved Grandparents

Bishop John G. and Lady Clora D. Thompson, although you both are no longer with me in the natural, your spirit lives on within me. Thank you from the very deeps for embracing me as your daughter and loving me in all the ways Christ has loved. I will forever be grateful to God for placing me on your hearts and becoming everything that I would need in later years to come. From a child, you saw the gifts and talents on my life and spoke greatness continually upon it. You both showed me how to be strong and stand firm against all obstacles. Thank you, dad and mom. I love and miss you deeply.

To My Beloved Mother

Mommy Christine L. Thompson, you saw the artistry and poet long before I could understand it. You would call me your artistic daughter; I still can hear your voice in the winds. Lovely in all your ways, you saw yourself imperfect, but you were perfect for me. Thank you for teaching me the secret in laughter. little did I know it would be the laughter that changed my perceptive on people in life

ABOUT THE AUTHOR

Tracy Norris is a writer with a strong background in performing arts based in Columbus, OH. She is the mother of two extraordinary boys that she calls her heavyweight champions! She allows her poetry to empower and encourage people by sharing her story through writing. Her message to all is, "WHAT DIDN'T KILL ME ONLY MADE ME STRONGER!"

Tracy found her true essence by embracing herself whole heartily and releasing it back to others. Your voice has the power to change, unlock, and release others to their purpose.

It's within the pages upon your heart, let it speak, The Essence of Life, Open Love Letters.

f facebook.com/tnorris03

www.ingramcontent.com/pod-product-compliance
Lightning Source LLC
Chambersburg PA
CBHW030154100526
44592CB00009B/272